There has been a time when…perhaps the
esteem of the world was of higher value in my
eye than everything in it. But age, experience, and
reflection, preserving to that only its due value,
have set a higher on tranquility.

Mr. Jefferson's Upland Virginia

LIBRARY OF CONGRESS CATALOG NUMBER: 83-050396
HARDCOVER ISBN: 0-934738-06-8   SOFTCOVER ISBN: 0-934738-07-6
PRINTED AND BOUND IN JAPAN BY DAI NIPPON PRINTING CO., LTD.
FIRST PUBLISHED IN 1979 BY UPLAND PUBLISHING, INC.
SECOND PRINTING IN 1983 BY THOMASSON-GRANT, INC.,
2250-6 OLD IVY ROAD, CHARLOTTESVILLE, VIRGINIA 22901, (804) 977-1780.

Mr. Jefferson's Upland Virginia

A Photographic Celebration of Thomas Jefferson's Homeland

PHOTOGRAPHY BY ROBERT LLEWELLYN

SELECTIONS FROM THE WRITINGS OF THOMAS JEFFERSON

Thomas Jefferson is Upland Virginia's most renowned native. He was born in 1743 at Shadwell, an outpost on the Virginia frontier, beyond the navigable reaches of the rivers, where settlers shared the territory with packs of hunting wolves, Indians, and occasionally, a wandering bison. The ancient Blue Ridge, rising in the haze to the West, was forested with massive chestnut trees, many of them twice the girth of the hardwoods covering the slopes today.

This primitive place had a profound effect upon Jefferson. Although much of his youth was spent to the East, in the more settled area of Tuckahoe Plantation on the James River, Jefferson's mind and heart turned often to his native Albemarle County. The region was wild and vast, offering the freedom and space for intelligence and courage to fill it. And it could not have been lost upon the young classical scholar that in mythology mountains served as the throne of the gods.

Public life frequently called him away, yet Jefferson began as a young gentleman farmer to build his mansion, Monticello, on a peak overlooking the Blue Ridge Mountains. He also maintained property to the South, at Poplar Forest in Bedford County, near Natural Bridge. His curiosity with natural science and his devotion to his native region led him to write *Notes on the State of Virginia*, a unique commentary on the flora, fauna, and population of the province. After a long and distinguished public career, he retired to his mountaintop home to pursue his loves, science and gardening. In retirement he performed his last great service to his native state and to his country. He founded, designed, and oversaw the construction of the first buildings of the University of Virginia.

It was William Howard Taft who commented on a visit to Charlottesville that people still spoke of "Mr. Jefferson" as though he were in the next room. Many still do. So we call this book *Mr. Jefferson's Upland Virginia*, since the region in so many ways belongs to him. Surely his spirit abides here, delights in the mountain brooks and morning mists on rivers, the endless song of mockingbirds, the silent grace of wildflowers in the forests. We offer the second printing of this book as a celebration of the indomitable spirit of the man and the incomparable beauty of the region he loved.

Charlottesville, 1983

The first glance of this scene hurries our senses into the opinion that this earth has been created in time, that the mountains were formed first, that the rivers began to flow afterwards...

I hold (without appeal to revelation) that when we take a view of the universe, in its parts, general or particular, it is impossible for the human mind not to perceive and feel a conviction of design, consummate skill, and indefinite power in every atom of its composition. The movements of the heavenly bodies, so exactly held in their course by the balance of centrifugal and centripetal forces; the structure of our earth itself, with its distribution of lands, waters, and atmosphere; animal and vegetable bodies, examined in all their minutest particles; insects, mere atoms of life, yet as perfectly organized as man or mammoth; the mineral substances, their generation and uses; it is impossible, I say, for the human mind not to believe that there is in all this design, cause, and effect up to an ultimate cause, a Fabricator of all things from matter and motion, their Preserver and Regulator.

On the whole I find nothing anywhere else in point of climate which Virginia need envy to any part of the world....When we consider how much climate contributes to the happiness of our condition, by the fine sensation it excites, and the productions it is the parent of, we have reason to value highly the accident of birth in such a one as that of Virginia.

The earth belongs to the living, not to the dead. The will and the power of man expire with his life, by nature's law....Each generation has the usufruct of the earth during the period of its continuance. When it ceases to exist, the usufruct passes on to the succeeding generation, free and unencumbered....

My history…would have been as happy a one as I could have asked could the objects of my affection have been immortal. But all the favors of fortune have been embittered by domestic losses. Of six children I have lost four, and finally their mother.

For the mountain being cloven asunder, she presents to your eye, through the cleft, a small catch of smooth blue horizon, at an infinite distance in the plain country, inviting you, as it were, from the riot and tumult roaring around, to pass through the breach and participate of the calm below....This scene is worth a voyage across the Atlantic...

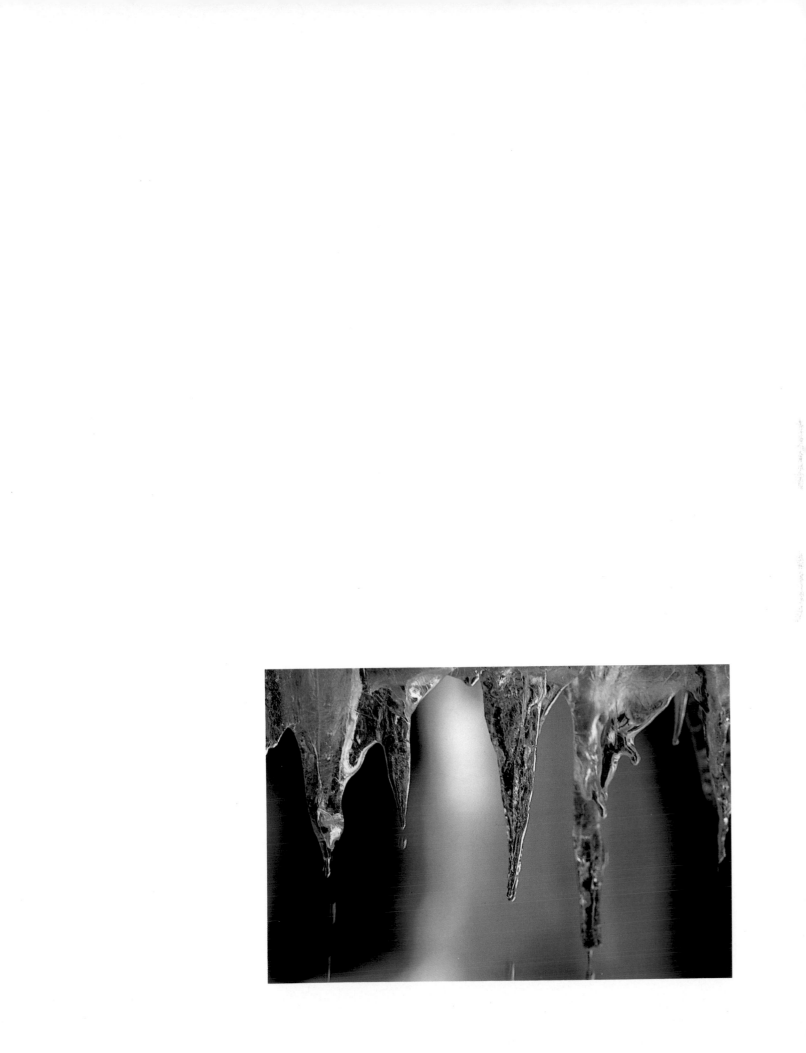

In a life where we are perpetually exposed to want and accident, yours is a wonderful proposition, to insulate ourselves, to retire from all aid, and to wrap ourselves in the mantle of self-sufficiency! For, assuredly, nobody will care for him who cares for nobody. But friendship is precious, not only in the shade but in the sunshine of life; and thanks to a benevolent arrangement of things the greater part of life is sunshine.

I have often thought that if heaven had given me choice of my position and calling, it should have been on a rich spot of earth, well watered, and near a good market for the productions of the garden. No occupation is so delightful to me as the culture of the earth, and no culture comparable to that of the garden. Such a variety of subjects, some one always coming to perfection, the failure of one thing repaired by the success of another, and instead of one harvest a continued one through the year. Under a total want of demand except for our family table, I am still devoted to the garden. But though an old man, I am but a young gardener.

This country...is red and hilly...excellently adapted to wheat, maize, and clover; like all mountainous countries it is perfectly healthy....The society is much better than is common in country situations; perhaps there is not a better country society in the United States....It consists of plain, honest, and rational neighbors, some of them well informed and men of reading, all superintending their farms, hospitable and friendly.

Those who labor in the earth are the chosen people of God, if ever He had a chosen people, whose breasts He has made His peculiar deposit for substantial and genuine virtue.

The most fortunate of us, in our journey through life, frequently meet with calamities and misfortunes which may greatly afflict us, and to fortify our minds against the attacks of these calamities and misfortunes should be one of the principal studies and endeavors of our lives. The only method of doing this is to assume a perfect resignation to the Divine Will, to consider that whatever does happen, must happen; and that, by our uneasiness, we cannot prevent the blow before it does fall, but we may add to its force after it has fallen.

When I recollect that at fourteen years of age the whole care and direction of myself was thrown on myself entirely...and recollect the various sorts of bad company with which I associated from time to time, I am astonished I did not turn off with some of them and become as worthless to society as they were....From the circumstances of my position I was often thrown into the society of horse racers, card players, fox hunters, scientific and professional men, and of dignified men; and many a time have I asked myself in the enthusiastic moment of the death of a fox, the victory of a favorite horse, the issue of a question eloquently argued at the bar or in the great council of the nation, well, which of these kinds of reputations should I prefer? That of a horse jockey? a fox hunter? an orator? or the honest advocate of my country's rights?

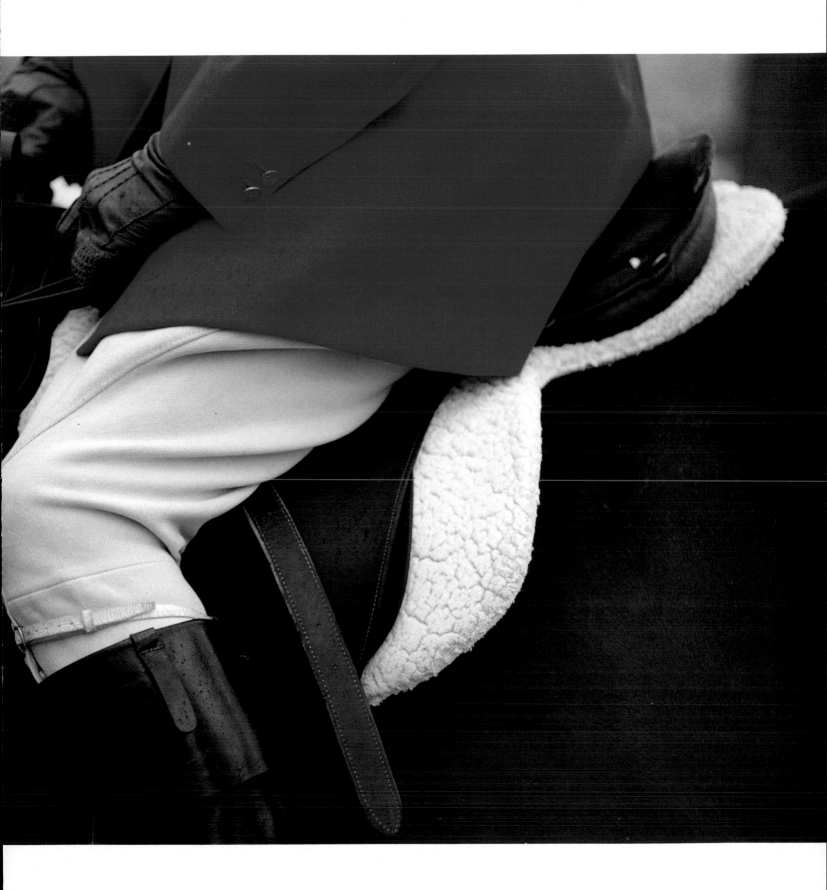

Everything in this world is a matter of calculation. Advance then with caution, the balance in your hand. Put into one scale the pleasures which any object may offer; but put fairly into the other the pains which are to follow, and see which preponderates. The making of an acquaintance is not a matter of indifference. When a new one is proposed to you, view it all round. Consider what advantages it presents, and to what inconveniences it may expose you. Do not bite at the bait of pleasure till you know there is no hook beneath it. The art of life is the art of avoiding pain; and he is the best pilot who steers clearest of the rocks and shoals with which it is beset. Pleasure is always before us, but misfortune is at our side; while running after that, this arrests us.

The Creator has made the earth for the living, not the dead. Rights and powers can only belong to persons, not to things.... A generation may bind itself as long as its majority continues in life; when that has disappeared, another majority is in place...and may change their laws and institutions to suit themselves. Nothing then is unchangeable but the inherent and unalienable rights of man.

Every government degenerates when
trusted to the rulers of the people alone.
The people themselves therefore are its only
safe depositories. And to render even them
safe, their minds must be improved to a
certain degree.

The University will give employment to my remaining years, and quite enough for my senile faculties. It is the last act of usefullness I can render, and could I see it open I would not ask an hour more of life.

History by apprizing (students) of the past will enable them to judge of the future; it will avail them of the experience of other times and other nations; it will qualify them as judges of the actions and designs of men; it will enable them to know ambition under every disguise it may assume, and, knowing it, to defeat its views.

Withdrawn by age from all other public services and attentions to public things, I am closing the last scenes of life by fashioning and fostering an establishment for the instruction of those who are to come after us. I hope its influence on their virtue, freedom, fame, and happiness will be salutary and permanent.

Exercise and recreation...are as necessary as reading; I will say rather more necessary, because health is worth more than learning. A strong body makes the mind strong....The object of walking is to relax the mind. You should therefore not permit yourself even to think while you walk; but divert yourself by the objects surrounding you. Walking is the best possible exercise.

I am as happy nowhere else, and in no other society, and all my wishes end, where I hope my days will, at Monticello. Too many scenes of happiness mingle themselves with all the recollections of my native woods and fields to suffer them to be supplanted in my affection by any other.

We hold these truths to be self-evident: that all men are created equal; that they are endowed by their Creator with (inherent and) certain inalienable rights; that among these are life, liberty, and the pursuit of happiness.

PASSAGES were selected from Thomas Jefferson's correspondence and public writings:

PHOTOGRAPHS were taken throughout Upland Virginia, including the following historical sites: